WORDS ON

Printed in the United Kingdom
First Printing, 2025
ISBN: 978-1-0683520-1-0

WORDS ON

words on grief
written in the days,
weeks and months
following my
husband's Stage IV
metastatic cancer
diagnosis

Sara Tetlow

DEDICATION

To Ollie, Cora and Charlie,
may you always inspire hope
and prevent sleep.

WORDS ON

WORDS ON GRIEF & GRATITUDE

we watch others
go over challenge
and through tragedy

hoping it
skips a beat
and forgets
to land on us

but it does

nothing
makes it better
except one tether

knowing there's
someone
somewhere

who's aftermath
is our very path

and we sink

and we rise

on wobbly legs
we pick ourselves up
and reach
for those in front

to share the brunt
and ease the pain

and we thrive

collecting
knowledge
and grit
experience
and perseverance

and we help

passing hope
to those behind
we have yet
to find

written for those who hold us up and for those we'll hold up next

WORDS ON SHOCK

are you there

thankfully there's
a planet under me

standing on my own
like we're supposed to
isn't meant to be

where do you go
when you're not here

to the stars
to the sea
to the wind
to the trees

they say your
senses help
but what if
they ran

skipped town
for a while
while the heart
decides if it can

taste forgot
to matter
numb replaced touch

pound
pound
pound
is the only sound

i keep looking
but there's
nothing to see
smell is overwhelming me

stay for a while
in your head

the lights will
come on
when you
least expect

am i here

are you there

i am here

you are here

written while laying in the grass in a London park

WORDS ON DENIAL

everyone is running in mud

who has the patience
to wait
for someone
with time
without a push
to find
efficient rhyme

who lets the day
take you
where you
need to be
and forget
the list of me

it's a luxury
to wait
to meander
along the street

and watch
the clouds
roll past

to stop
for a chat
or a second
skinny flat

everyone has
a place to be

an hour to shower
a moment to keep
a long list
lost on repeat

food is happenstance
a romance
lost in the cracks
between
utility

keep up
there's always
the next

do you maintain
that monotony
staves off reality

or complain
that aspiration
doesn't move
the same
as perspiration

written after small talk at a school event

WORDS ON FRUSTRATION

why are thoughts
like wind
but words
like weights

i love writing
but i hate writing this

you can't see
the seesaw
i'm stuck in my head
confined to my law

why can we
so easily look
but never see
looking is so easy
involuntary

but even the things
we see just beyond
our lashes and toes

are reserved for those
whose lives carry on

they probably don't
still
it doesn't change
the view

people say
my coattails
hang on hope
and magic

but truth is
i hate inspiration motivation
i hate onwards backwards

i hate resilient helpless
i hate joy sad

i hate hope despair
i hate yesterday now

i hate forever

most of all
i hate the carefree
that was taken
by the wind
to a place
i’ll never be

i wonder who
is breathing in
that part of me

will i ever
get to see

written while sitting in Brockwell Park trying something new to cope

WORDS ON ANGER

anger is
a funny feel
it starts
as whispers
nothing real

clenching fists
and furrowed brows
show what's in
is out

a rumble and a pop
as bubbles make
their way up top

to gather 'round
a heated space
to say their peace
and take their place

jaws rise
and find their friends
who clench down
and make amends

trying with all
their might
to convince words
and thoughts
to hang on tight

everything
that slips away
will make it
to another day

but those stuck
just below the crust
are bound to create
such a fuss

that over time
all that helps

is
an
explosion

nothing
else

written while in my office working out contingency plan number five

WORDS ON GUILT

how long
do we have
to do the tasks
we should amass

to say the things
we didn't say
to look around
and say we'll stay

do decisions
come or go
i wish i knew
if faster is better
or longer is foe

the saying goes
be grateful
for another day

a chance to say
the things we may
have stored
because the last time
was ignored

but if you had
just one more day

to watch
the sunrise
disappear

to listen
to the voice
that keeps
your melody
by ear

to touch
a heart
or a stem

to feel
the hand
of the only man

to smell
lingering
goodbyes

to find
the taste
that sends
memories
to your eyes

would you choose
the very best

or would you simply
lie down and rest

written at two am after trying and failing to sleep

WORDS ON WHY ME

what do you do
where do you start
when you don't know
who to call or
why me

searching
for anything
to make the non
sense make
sense

and take the fury
from the jury
who decide
yes
she's the one

who can
find the path
do the math
take the chance

do the things
that take more
than their fair share
of a person's
life or air

lost to the idea
that anyone
can come to feel

an inkling
of the duration
of frustration

that lingers
when the very squall
laid out for you

is
just
begging
you
to
fall

written while waiting in reception to collect my son

WORDS ON ENDURANCE

someone asked me
how i do it
you're such a warrior
you always rise

but warrior applies
only to those
who create war
have experience
will fight

a war against who
against what
until when
for how long

where's muscle
memory from
if there's no memory
and no muscle

simply hired
for a career
with no idea

will fight won't fight
can't fight should fight
please fight must fight
let's fight we'll fight

warriors get to keep
soulmates as mates
and not souls

they get to begin
again with we
they don't wait and see

today i heard it
slip away
through wobbly
ears and tears

where does
out of body go
it dances on rainbows
before it goes on
the only way it knows

in the haze
when I couldn't recall
if our life
made its way
to a wonderwall

i held on for dear life
staying just
within reach
to consider
the breach

someone asked me
how i do it

the summit paints
my portrait

written at midday while sitting on my favorite bench in Dulwich Village

WORDS ON HEARTBREAK

it starts in the heart
where the beat
keeps time with time
where lives roll on
where love lives

a forgotten tap-tap
when the world
is as it aught to be

not fighting for life
gasping for air
surveying the unfair

inside the complex life
of hearts on strike

not aware
it should be
involuntary
to centre the world
and ease the strain

a simple shape
switches off
to remind us
it's all temporary

that's when
the heart stalls
beating against
imaginary walls

skipping not
from love sent
but from the pain
of what was
never meant

a heart breaks

it calls for help
to rush
before the skip
becomes too much

and pounding starts
in all the spokes
a call again
there must be hope

a mind of popped fun
lungs fight
against no one
joints despair
and muscles ache

breathe they say
it's just a mistake

brought on
because
even fighters
need a break

written at midnight while watching my husband breathe in sleep

WORDS ON SADNESS

afraid of tears
who holds
your fears
who takes a peek
into your soul
and decides to stay
and not to go

when broken glass
and sorrows creep
when ages pass
into the deep

what do we do
when all that's left
of happy thoughts

are a smile's descent
into the place
where sadness goes
to where it's meant

it hollows out
the happiest place
burrows into
muscles deep

it tells a heart
to forget to beat
and moves the body
off its feet

it stays a while and keeps
a different seat

always a reminder
of too much to bear

a chair
meant for
love and hope
falls from
certainty to cope

without a net
to catch our years

we stand beside
our hopes
and fears
and watch
our happy
disappear

this is why
i'm afraid of tears

written before Friday family movie night (Ken's Fish & Chips & Minions)

WORDS ON LONELINESS

who comes to help
when those that held us
up and down
decide to go away

to pack their promises
and could-haves
and take what's
left of the day

who breaks up
before down
and makes a choice
to hold their heart
in their own hands

to keep it safe
and sent away
and mend
the broken seams

who grows up and out
and takes up space
that was always kept
for someone else

to learn from years
of little steps
that lead right
back to us

who comes to see
what's in between
the heartbreak
and the calm

that takes the place
of could-have-beens
and holds them
in their palms

to love the person
we've become
when someone
else has left

has got to be
the greatest gift
to never leave
the nest

a reminder
that the person
who always comes
is best

written while rubbing my son's back at bedtime

WORDS ON PANIC

to stop or start
to stay or go
to be or not
to drop

one foot in front
of another foot
to a place
where feelings
come and go
and no one knows

where headaches loop
and shoulders droop
eyes swoop
and bodies stoop

lungs at attention
from bodies
lost in motion

and brains
on third, fourth
hundredth tries
to make sense
of worlds and dreams
gone by

to stay or go
to sit and be
to forget and urge
the past to flee

or stay and free
the broken thoughts
to let them out
from eyes and ears
from mouths and tears

to float among
the other things
that seem to have
a different scene

to stay and go
is all I know

and sometimes
when my brain
does both
when my body tries
to drown and float

i find the will
to balance
in the in between

to stay to go
to know

that one day
all the friction ends

with acceptance
of the might-have-beens

written while crouched on the floor of the Tate Modern avoiding a panic attack

WORDS ON INSOMNIA

what to do
when thoughts
race to nowhere
and dreams
dance on repeat

fingers and toes
and nose
move with
restless abandon
searching
for something
that's already lost

words come
but mostly go
stuck in between
daydreams and sleep
nightmares and fear

in the quiet
of the middle
of the dark part
of the day
nothing rests

eyes dart
back and forth
up and down
round
and round
and round

then bile rises
and thunder hides
behind eyes

muscles try
to unravel
past mistakes
while every
joint aches

open eyes
bring calm
before the storm
that sits
behind lids

then wide screens
become sleepy
skinny slits

when did sleep
escape
to far off places
with no
end date

written while sleeping in my garden under the stars avoiding claustrophobia

WORDS ON DISSOCIATION

slow motion
no motion
commotion

blurry lines
and hazy eyes
colours seep
together
under dim lights
and lashed lids

chatter starts
and stops
and lips move
but no one
speaks

the buzz and bops
on tabletops
make a beat

the hum carries a tune
i try to remember
but can only
remember
i forgot to repeat

surely if i move a bit
get up and wander
my force will recall
the time before
i sat behind this wall

i used to dictate
connect the dreams
between seats

string them along
from plate to plate
watch laughter bounce
on glass rims
and treats

i used to create
moments that move
from place to place
person to person

the perfect seat
or repeat
or pause
or cause

moments still join
finding a clasp
when they fit the gist

but those days
are meant
for someone else

mine
only
twist

written after dinner at the Chiltern Firehouse with an old friend

WORDS ON STAYING PRESENT

please just stay
just stay here
right here
in the second
that past

the last
time i tried to stay
it only served to cast
a long dark
shadow past

why can't i stay
right here

my brain takes off
to elsewhere

high-aboves
or down-belows
to decades gone
and never knows

please just stay
just stay here
right here

let's put something
in the way
a book
a brick
a memory

nothing stops
the past
from leaping
over present

to invent stories
that end in ways
we know
we'll never know

they write rhymes
and sorrowful
goodbyes

they push
past bends
refusing to rest
until they've
met their end

please just stay
just stay here
right here

for today

written while sitting in a closet crying so my children wouldn't see

WORDS ON UNPREDICTABILITY

one moment or second
makes or breaks me
or maybe
it just takes me
to a place
i never needed to go

day to day
happens
day to day
get up
coffee pot
catch train
miss stop
dodge rain

a million pivotal
decisions
to get to one
that creeps
around corners
like hoarders

taking things in stride
but never knowing
if the ride
is worth
the anticipate

then the moment
comes or goes
and drums loud or soft

to welcome in
the newest life
of hope
or nope
not yet

we wait and wait
for things
to culminate

not as we hoped
they would
but just so that
we know we could
live to last
another day

to observe
the other way
it could have gone

if the day to day
brought us through
a different before

not this one

that we never
ever
chose to
explore

written in the waiting room while my husband had his third CT scan

WORDS ON APATHY

how tight
can you hold on
to nothing

can you
wrap up hope
or spend time
with memory

do thoughts
and ideas
drape over a chair

when everyone
out there
keeps trying
to find

the right hook
the right scene
the right corner
to hang a dream

if you squeeze
does it pop

will it ebb
and flow
until no one
knows
exactly where
it's been

is it out of the way
is it the way

watch it escape
and wander
to and fro
back and forth
along the inside

around
and around
it goes

still
i have
no interest
in what
it knows
and shows

written at midnight on a Tuesday before chemotherapy

WORDS ON GIVING UP

i cannot go on like this
this doesn't work
not any of it

not the part
that pretends
to spin plates
end-on-end
nor the part
that shows up early
and smiles
for the surly

nor the one who says
ah, i'll never rest
rest is for the weary
and the dreary

maybe it's in jest
but really
it's just a way
to explain the stress

god the days
are long
and hard
and dreadful

what keeps us in song
what's the point
of moving forward
to find laughs

when every smile
moves toward
insatiable
backdrafts

so do we give up
or do we give

until every inch
of body mind and soul
is plucked apart
to fill
a casted role

keep the others
going strong

morph into a prong
that serves to hold
another's heart
but doesn't
quite belong

and when we gently
whisk away
and find unexpectedly
that there's
nothing left to see

is it then that we give up
or try again to be

written while sitting on my bathroom floor crying from exhaustion

WORDS ON DEPRESSION

if i could see it
i would move it

take it by
the hand
and lead it
elsewhere
anywhere

to sit it down
and have a chat

to please stop
coming over
when the balance
has been met

when no one
calls your name

or invites
your kind of flame
to gather
above the air
that feels light
everywhere

move along
to shelters
that will keep
you safe

there you'll find
the other heavys
that are also
out of place

you can have
whatever
you need

just
take
your
weight
and
dagger
and
find
someone
else's
free

written while trying to convince myself to go see DJ Annie Mac

WORDS ON BREAKING

is it better
to crack
with ease
or speed

to shatter
or eek
across a sheet
to snap
or pop
or slowly drop

one rebounds
with such force
the pain shocks
down with
no remorse

while others
come in
from the side
a slow dull ache
that tries to hide

until all at once
it seems the bite
did break a seam
that bleeds out
across a dream

both shake shake
and ask for more
waiting
to be adored

to break right down
to the floor

to wait
for whispers
and encores

the mystery
beneath
drives
gazers wild
with curiosity
so deep

it begs
the question
on repeat

who missed
the leak

written while in a car park after ten months of trying not to break

WORDS ON LIFE BEFORE

i forgot today
for as long
as it took
to remember

progress
or peace
or neither
of those

maybe just
the top
of a summit
or bottom
of who-knows

blue eyes and
sad goodbyes

no

blue eyes
and always tries

written while waiting to collect my daughter from school

WORDS ON STRENGTH

so many but only
a few make it

to be anything more
than hidden
underneath

at a depth so deep
in the rough

everlasting just
undercover

seek and find
find and seek
on repeat

are we all stronger
than a million
thought-we-mays
sorry-can't-stays

only a few make it

but those that do
sit atop a pedestal view
of strength and beauty
shining unconditional love

a promise to always
find light
in the tough

written for a dear friend while riding in a London taxi

WORDS ON BELONGING

by the time
you've gone
around the block
stacked
the decades
and took stock
of all the different
shades

do your labels
find the others
or have you made
your own way

do you belong
to who you were
way back when

or do you compare
to all the stairs
you took to reach
the zen

does the earth
that held your tiny feet
remind you
it always repeats

or are the places
that were trodden last
the ones that shape
the looking glass

when you have moved
amongst the seas
and picked up pieces
that became like me

do the parts
that make the whole
mean you belong
to something more

or is your jigsaw
just for you
which means
it's only one of two

belonging
becomes
the person
you choose
to weather
all the time
with you

written while sitting in the dark after my family fell asleep

WORDS ON HOPE

what happens
to the air
when the fear's
not there

when hope pierces
all the pain
with a blinding reign

does it hide
around the bend
knocking on doors
helping
dreams end

or does it collect
more of itself
and make its way
to someone else

does it sift
and stir
instigating
worlds of folklore
based half on facts
and half on tour

the air changes
to a sheen
that reminds us
of the perfect scene

where fear
is packed
into particles
that float

so freely
in the air
that we forget
to stare

and all
at once
they're up
up
up
not down

designed
to go
up and out
and orbit 'round
the universe

they watch
and try to
be let in

but our air
is christening

written at 3am the night before chemo cycle 18

WORDS ON FRIENDSHIP

valleys are low and slow
deep and narrow
long and gradual

in them sits
dark drowning days
with sleep in jest
poking at a great unrest

we look up
to the highest rim
the edge of life or hope

but even with the biggest push
the greatest team
the largest rope

the chance of ever
getting there
to see the peaks
and meet the weeks
seems something
out of neverland

so there we sit
and do our best
to prop us up
and bear the test

then roundabout
the time we break
when valleys are
the deepest deep

we look to see
a ray of light
fall down from
the highest flight

a friend a chat
a hopeful pat
a challenge
that we've never had

a person who
has gone before

a dewy glimpse
of something more

the rim that sat
so far away
dips down
to show us
there's a way

to crawl inside
the shielded space
that holds our heart
and keeps the pace

every valley
has a way
to see the sun
meet another day

written while on a sunny dog walk in London

WORDS ON RESILIENCE

facial muscles
make it
but really lifetimes do
what a peculiar clue

fake ones seem real
and real ones are fake
at least for me
they are now

an expectation
of white teeth
and grin lines
smize and an all's well
that ends

well
why do those
that freely
give it away
end up paying
for it later

forcing a face
for the sake of it
then for the same sake
doing it all over again

little lifelines
make different shapes
than long lifetimes

yet those should have
enough actual joy
to fill a thousand crescents

what's in a smile

it's hope that bobs
on heartache seas
a fake-it please believe me

acknowledging you know
without saying it's so
the hint of old memories
anticipation
of a moment in time
that's better than
a moment in plan

an invisible string
through a hard goodbye
humour in sync
an unconditional link

how lucky are we
that our corners
creep up
and won't give up

even when
everything's
crumbling down

written after an aimless walk and cry with my best friend

WORDS ON FAITH

ripples run
like tiptoes walk
down backs
and decades

rings of fire
and despair
of loneliness
and nearly there

a deed undone
just like i knew
you'd never come

one
two two
three three three
and off concentric circles go

to cast a gaze
a glance a look
along a life
well lived
but not always
by the book

where do ripples run
and who from
where do ripples go
to and from

one and only one

and here i stand
the beginning
and the end

of all the memories
we keep

dreams of could haves
should haves
must haves

the center of a wave
that comes and goes
as we behave

sometimes like
we learned
before we knew the way
would only ever
come to pass

one and only one day

we find the highest peaks
and plunge
into the valleys

those who look
from afar to see

will never be
as strong as me

written before bed while feeling like my old self for a day

WORDS ON FLEXIBILITY

do feathers have a role
when not connected
to a wing

or do they simply
float in the wind
waiting for
a gust or breeze
or rain to soak
their dreams

when the rush
picks up
and meets
another draft
what happens
to the long-planned path

does it continue on
until the end
or try to finish
force the plan
not to diminish

a seesaw
of back and forth
to and fro
should i stay or go

until the tick-tock clock
moves right not left
up not down

forward no wait
go back
begin again

it settles
in the path
waiting until
the last blows pass

when the feather
finally departs
when blistering winds
stop pulling it apart

does it get to rest
on grasses wet
or does it slip
between
the cracks
and get stuck
with no impact

it floats and drifts
to the ground

where soon it's bound
to meet the next storm
to come around

written while sitting in the car after cancelling plan A, again

WORDS ON ACCEPTANCE

everything can wait
for a time when waiting
is everything

fluffy pops
of bespoke air
climb up to find
spare space

before they disappear
to a place
where no one goes
they've lost
their grace

in the middle
of the skies
everything
that lies
amidst the molecules
of lives
and misty hopes
that could settle
in long strands
but choose
instead fate

is a reminder

that everything

will wait

clouds wait for wind
to blow them
to the next best place

seeds wait
for rain and sun
and sun and rain

while sand takes shape
to hope for waters
that escape
to force it yet again to wait

sun waits
for the moon
while stars
wait for the dark
morning
waits for dew
twilight
waits for you

remember always
that everything
can wait

until waiting in the wings
in the uncomfortable space
that lies between

is actually everything

written from the front room after choosing rest over dishes

WORDS ON THE FUTURE

golden hour
is the most
magnificent

right before
the sun rests
when the world
turns away
from the day

joy and misery
pushed from reality
to memory
by billions of years
of remedy

that light
for just a second
renders everything
aureate

water sparkles gold
and tree tops
carry crowns tenfold

faces flooded
with beams
just soft enough
to stay and see

My Heart reminds me
it's free

usually we cast
that hour aside
before night falls
into twilight
midnight
stars
sunrise

you sleep
alongside
but i don't
i wait

until the golden hour
hits its stride

saving the last ray
to spark a new tide

we'll be ok
day after day

if we
can
just
hold
onto
the
gold

written after watching the sunset from Telegraph Hill, London

WORDS ON LOVE

love arrives swiftly
by taking you out
by forcing a stop
right before the swap
would send you
into an abyss
unsaved by a kiss

it picks you up
from panic
on no conditions
but to be your manic

it tags in
when you're done
when the relentless
comes on

and sends
your usual calm
to places you
didn't know
you're free to go

it only judges
when you ask
or when it comes
too close to know
that if it didn't
check your breath
you'd find the others
had already left

it pulls up chairs
and opens doors

and makes the choices
but don't despair

it always takes
into account
the partner
that has been
left out

unconditional
is larger than
the next date or trek

it's quite simply
respect

when the lights go out
and no one's left
when dreams
are dashed
and we start
from scratch

the only person
you would choose
is the one
you'd die
to lose

written while on a twilight walk around my block

AUTHOR'S NOTE

'Please come straight away.
I have incurable cancer.'

I never expected these words to leave my 40-year-old husband's mouth when he rang me from the hospital in February 2024.

In the time that followed, grief took over regardless of my desire to endure. The single thing that continues to help our family fight Stage IV bowel cancer is knowing that someone, somewhere has already made our journey.

We find immense comfort in finding stories of acceptance, resilience, perseverance and ultimately, hope.

This poetry collection marries words and emotions. My hope is that by sharing my *Words On* grief, many of which were written in the brightest and darkest times (and in some odd places!), it eases my anguish and yours, too, no matter what you're trudging through.

Keep going.

THOUGHTS

THOUGHTS

THOUGHTS

THOUGHTS

THOUGHTS

Printed in Great Britain
by Amazon

60579068R00047